Winning with Freelancers

REMOTE iT!

MICHAEL BROOKS

Entrepreneur and industry-leading CEO

**Build and manage a thriving
business in a virtual world**

goLance, Inc.

Dover, Delaware

This publication is designed to educate and provide general
information. It is not intended to replace the counsel of other
professional experts, such as business coaches, accountants,
human resource professionals, and other advisers. Readers
are encouraged to consult with their own advisers regarding
specific situations. While the author has taken reasonable
precautions in the preparation of this book and believes the
facts presented within the book are accurate, the author, editors, and publisher (goLance, Inc.) assume no responsibility
for errors or omissions. The author, editors, and publisher
(goLance, Inc.) specifically disclaim any liability resulting
from the use or application of the information contained in
this book.

Names and identifying details have been changed to protect
the privacy of individuals.

goLance, Inc.
8 The Green, Suite 4753
Dover, Delaware 19901

golance.com

Because of the dynamic nature of the Internet, any web ad-
dresses or links contained in this book may have changed
since publication and may no longer be valid.

REMOTE iT!: Winning with Freelancers / Michael Brooks – 1st
edition.
ISBN 978-1-7354749-1-5 paperback
ISBN 978-1-7354749-0-8 ebook
Library of Congress Control Number: 2020917895

This book is dedicated to freelancers and entrepreneurs who are changing the way the world works.

Contents

Introduction **1**
    Remote Culture 4
    The Remote Culture Differentiator 7

1: Growing Your Business
with Freelance Talent 11
    The Old 9-to-5 12
    Freelancer Benefits 14
    Why Hire Freelancers? 15
    Common Reasons for Using Freelancers 18
    Freelancers Versus Big Agencies 20
    Establish Two-Way Trust 23

2: Hiring and Managing a World-Class Team.... 27
    Making the Leap 27
    FAQs About Hiring Freelancers 29
    Verifying the Freelancer 33
    Special Tips for Startups 35
    Start on the Right Foot 36
    Funding Options 38
    Common Misunderstandings 39
    Identify Preferred Platforms 40
    What to Ask in an Interview 43
    Non-disclosure Agreements (NDAs) 49

3: Managing Diverse Skill Sets 51
    Set Realistic Expectations 51
    Be Available, Timely, and Responsive 54

4: Creating a Great Culture in a Virtual World.. 57
    Culture Matters 57
    Culture by Choice or Circumstance? 60
    Why You Need a Suitable Culture Fit 61
    Thoughtful Hiring and Training 62
    Team Meetings and One-on-Ones 64

Remote Appreciation Tips................................... 66
The "goCulture" Approach 68
Right Tools for the Right People 69
Remote Corporate Retreats 71
In-Person Visits 72
Write Your Own Rules..................................... 73
Test Your Culture 74

**5: Moving from Skype to Zoom to 3D Virtual
Meetings 81**
Remote Meeting Guidelines 81
Skype or Zoom? 84
The 3D Virtual World 85
Dynamic Written Collaboration.......................... 87

6: Building a Loyal Freelance Workforce.......... 89
The Power of Digital Friendships........................ 90
Five Minutes Before (and After) Meetings 92
Personalize Your Remote Visit........................... 92
Ten Ways to Increase Loyalty 93

7: Tackling Global Currency Challenges 95
Think Like a Freelancer 95
Flexible Payment Options 98

**8: Managing Remote Freelancers:
Case Studies 99**
Scale and Pay Quickly.................................... 100
Manage Remotely 102
Tackle Technical Limitations 103
Teamwork and Morale 104
Connect and Communicate 105
Cultural Issues 106

9: Leveraging Tools and Best Practices.......... 109
Evaluating Freelance Websites......................... 109
Legal and Ethical Responsibilities 112

Websites with International Freelancers 113
Effective Qualification Processes.......................115
Management and Payment Tools......................116

10: Trends in the Freelance Market 119
The Expanding Freelance Economy...................119
Future Impacts...121
A Change Is Coming......................................123
Conclusion 126

REMOTE iT! Checklist 129

REMOTE iT! Resources 135

Acknowledgments 137

About The Author 139

Other Books by Michael Brooks 141

Introduction

What does it take to "win" in business? It starts with having a great business model and a team of talented people to help your company scale and grow. You also need to adapt to changes that impact the economy, your market, and your workers.

The days of having people all together physically in the same office from Monday through Friday are no longer necessary for so many organizations. Many companies that didn't have remote policies until the COVID-19 pandemic occurred have told their people to work from home for a while. As a result, a variety of businesses have discovered the countless benefits of using a remote workforce. And there's no turning back.

If you're not using online freelance workers now, it's time to think about how they can help you meet your business objectives. When your business already leverages remote online freelance talent from the start, like mine, it helps to protect you from a wide range of disruptions that can impact your business. It can also enable you to reduce costs while meeting the demands of your customers.

To win in business, you also need a great corporate culture. Your freelancers should feel valued and connected with a shared vision, business model, and effective, intuitive tools to do their work remotely.

As the owner of a global online freelance marketplace, goLance, I've experienced the power of using talented remote workers to help build my business. I've also seen how an increased reliance upon online freelancers has offered so many companies the expertise they need to gain a competitive edge and grow their business, while also reducing overhead.

When I say, "winning with freelancers," I'm talking about achieving growth—blasting beyond your expectations to levels you've never imagined. I've done it, and so can you.

Here are some definitions to help you understand the concepts discussed in this book:

- *Global online freelance marketplace*: This is a place — a website — where businesses can find freelancers to do remote work from any location in the world, and freelancers can find jobs. The marketplace should offer a variety of services, such as the ability to screen, hire, verify, manage, track time, certify, and pay freelancers.

- *Freelance platform*: The marketplaces vary based on their business models, types of jobs they offer, features available, payment methods, and other capabilities. The platform supports the business model and includes a variety of software required to deliver services.

- *Online freelancers*: These are the people who can do their online jobs remotely, no matter where they are located. It can include people of all different skill sets, such as designers, writers, developers, customer service reps, virtual assistants, engineers, admins, SEO experts, email marketers, IT and administrators, and more.

For me, and the freelancers on my platform, freelancing equals freedom. Freelancing offers online workers and their clients the flexibility to work

3

from any location, and they often set their own hours. It also gives many options to business owners, who can reduce their overhead dramatically by cutting down on office space costs, infrastructure, maintenance, administrative functions, and more.

For example, I run a global business with about 550,000 users, and I expect it to reach 1,000,000 soon. I do all of this work directly from my home and don't have to fight traffic or commute. Instead, I use highly skilled online freelance talent from all over the world to deliver services to my company's clients. I'm living the dream. **As the freelance community continues to expand, business leaders must have the tools, processes, and passion to create a culture where their freelancers excel and deliver exceptional results.** When freelancers meet your performance objectives, your customers benefit from outstanding services—apps that work, intuitive websites, representatives that provide excellent customer experiences, speedy transactions, and more.

Remote Culture

A terrific remote culture shares and communicates the values of a business, which includes the company's vision and expectations of how free-lancers should interact with their managers and customers. It offers an environment that pro-motes creativity, innovation, communication, productivity, teamwork, and fun. By creating a culture that leverages best practices and technol-ogy for managing freelance talent, your company is well-positioned for growth.

I wrote this book to help share my experiences about how to hire, retain, and motivate freelancers in a changing world, where in-person, face-to-face meetings are a thing of the past.

I'll discuss strategies we've used to successfully embrace technology and provide a personal touch to reach our community while maintaining a happy, productive, global remote workforce. And we did this all while reducing costs. We've even held meetings in the 3-D world, which I confess started with me playing zombie games on Oculus Quest. More about that later.

At a time when Zoom has become a household word, and when people realize that they can ac-tually be more productive working remotely than in an office, the technology you use and the way you interact with your workforce can make the difference between success and failure. I've asked myself these questions:

- How can I build, grow, and manage a winning business with remote teams of freelancers?

- How can I have a virtual cup of coffee with them and have a chat with them?

- How can I experience who these freelancers are when they're thousands of miles away?

After asking these questions, I've discovered the answers, and you'll learn about them in this book. I care about the talented people who've helped to make my business grow, and that's the spirit that has driven the goLance culture since I first launched this online freelance marketplace in 2015. It's the same force that has helped my clients propel their businesses. I'll share some of my own experiences as well as examples of how clients have tackled some of their biggest challenges. Unless otherwise indicated, these examples are composites based on real-world situations.

Join me on this exciting journey to explore possibilities you may never have imagined. Learn about the tools and best practices available to help you build and navigate your way through growing and managing remote freelance teams that are becoming increasingly dependent on a virtual world.

How well you do is based on hiring the right talent, managing and connecting with them effectively, using the right technology, and being passionate about the vision for your business and the people who support it. Let this book be your guide!

The Remote Culture Differentiator

A remote culture is a way of working that's much different from what we've known in the past. Freelancers tend to work for a shorter duration than traditional employees. They may work for more than one business simultaneously. And they're often brought in to fill a role that's not available in-house. They're there for the project — not necessarily for many years, like people who work in traditional cultures.

Also, traditional businesses often have in-depth training programs, detailed documents describing their values, and have many long-term people who are very familiar with the organization's culture. However, with the right approach and freelance platform, it's amazing what you can accomplish with remote workers.

Some pundits predict that we're likely to witness the absolute domination of remote teams over fixed-office teams by 2025. In fact, a significant portion of our clients have businesses that are 100% freelance-based. Like me, their founders have built it from scratch. But there's a catch. Distributed teams just can't make things work effectively without a healthy culture. So, how can remote workers function as a team, as if they have shared the same office space for years, every single day, around the clock? Here are the essential strategies we'll discuss throughout the book:

- Choose the right corporate model.

- Generate an exceptional remote culture for your freelancers.

- Hire people with a wide range of different skill sets.

- Build a loyal workforce.

- Share the vision of your culture with free-lancers.

- Conduct productive meetings, possibly across multiple time zones.

- Leverage cutting-edge virtual collaboration tools.

- Use a freelance platform to recruit, screen, hire, manage, and pay workers.

- Understand how much money you can save with global freelance talent while achieving the results you expect.

By mastering these concepts, you too can win in business by using freelance talent.

chapter 1

Growing Your Business with Freelance Talent

I believe that one day in the not-so-distant future, nearly all of us will be freelancers. The thin line between the so-called "traditional" 9-to-5 and freelance jobs keeps becoming thinner. Many online freelancers work full-time, just like "regular" employees at traditional jobs. A key difference is that they work remotely and have more freedom and flexibility in their hours and choice of work.

Yes, it may seem like a big leap for most people to leave the perceived sense of security and stability in the traditional business world to freelance. But it can actually be a very positive shift. To tell you the truth, I don't even know what I really am these days. I used to be an employee. Then I become an entrepreneur. I spent time freelancing myself. Eventually, I launched a new freelance platform, goLance. So, I consider myself to be a freelancer/entrepreneur from head-to-toe.

Does everybody want to be a freelancer in today's economy? Not necessarily. Just like freelancing is all about freedom, I also believe that people have quite a few choices to make on their own. You've heard it so many times. "Freelancing is the future." But what's that supposed to mean?

Some people aren't even aware that they're freelancers. Some future generation, "xyz" or "zzz" — call it what you want — won't have a clue about the 9-to-5 world that once existed. They will be born in a new freelance economy, and they're going to like it. Think about it. It reminds me of how perception shifted after the iPhone was invented. People who have grown up with smartphones may not even realize that there was a time when only landlines were available, you couldn't take videos or pictures with a phone, and all you could do with a phone was make a call.

The Old 9-to-5

Let's examine the old standard of work and the new model to put freelancing into perspective. Traditional businesses hire employees who work for a specified period to complete a predetermined amount of work. Productivity is tracked through the impact and progress an employee provides. This cycle can become a dreaded routine for many people, even if the work they do is rewarding. It can look like this:

- Set the alarm.

- Wake up and get ready.

- Commute to work.

- Clock in. Work. Clock out.

- Commute home.

Since the 1950s, this has been the accepted standard. Today, however, working a traditional 9-to-5 job has become a 7:30 AM to 7:30 PM day, once you factor in getting ready, staying late, and commuting in traffic. The problem is that an employee is only paid for eight hours, but dedicates twelve hours a day to their job. That's only a 66% productivity rate at best.

What would happen if the standard could change? What if there were a way to increase the productivity of a worker by allowing more freedom while saving time and business expenses? Does this sound too good to be true? It's not.

Freelancer Benefits

Freelancers enjoy a very different lifestyle from in-office employees. Some of the benefits include:

- No obligation to wake up on a schedule because they may choose their own schedule based on what their clients require

- No commuting, which saves time and money — reducing traffic jams, parking fees, tolls, fuel costs, vehicle repairs, and auto insurance

- No maintenance or expenses for work clothes, uniforms, or having to dry clean business attire

- The ability to often choose which projects to work on, and when

- Freedom to manage their own time, with no permission required to run errands, or take care of family emergencies, reducing stress and anxiety — freelancers can clock in and out and have their time and work tracked to ensure they're meeting the expectations of their clients

- Holidays at the location of their choice, with no restrictions

- Pay that's relevant to skills, not set by an employer or corporate policy

- Ability to decide which projects to accept based on requirements and rates

- Ability to work on more than one contract at once, maximizing time management, improving productivity, and having the flexibility to expand their portfolio into new industries

- Excellent compensation based on experience, skills, and talents

The benefits employees gain from a job such as paid sick days, holidays, and vacations are all immediately offset by the control a freelancer has over time management. If freelancers don't want to work on Christmas, for instance, they can often extend work hours on the days preceding the holiday.

Why Hire Freelancers?

Here's a scenario that's all too common. Your company is getting off the ground and running. Profits are coming in, and you're relieved that your hard work is finally paying off. Then out of nowhere, a tragedy strikes. For example, think of the number of businesses that had to shut down or cut back dramatically because of the COVID-19 pandemic. Or, what if an employee quits or you must fire or dismiss someone to protect your business? Then business slows down, and your employees complain about their smaller paychecks. One of your top performers decides to leave. You're running short of staff and lost some of your greatest talent, and you need help to bounce back. Someone suggests you find a freelancer.

After hiring the freelancer, you discover that your business is back up-and-running smoothly again. You have no complaints and are satisfied with the work your freelancer produces. It suddenly strikes you that your employee expenses are lower, but you're paying the freelancer the same as your other employees. How did this happen?

One of the most significant benefits of hiring freelancers is that they are essentially self-employed and running their own businesses. That means that you can avoid paying:

- Payroll taxes

- Insurance expenses like medical, dental, and life

- Paid time off, such as vacations, sick days, and maternity/paternity leave

- Retirement, 401K, Worker's Compensation, and disability insurance

Freelancers should know the risks, the tax filing laws, and other associated legal concerns with their employment status. Freelancing is something that they chose. They are entrepreneurs on a path that no 9-to-5 job would have ever offered them. Besides saving money, what are some other benefits of hiring freelancers?

- Freelancers can be more flexible with their time. If they don't have to commute, they may be more likely to take an early-morning call if necessary.

- They tend to "live" for the project, as opposed to some employees who may work primarily out of obligation.

- Freelancers may be more likely to have multiple talents and skills in the areas you need.

- They are adaptable because they're used to working in different environments.

On average, freelancers have one to three contracts that they work on simultaneously. They have a level of enthusiasm and drive often unmatched in the traditional workforce. After all, if they don't get the results you're looking for, then they know they will be replaced. They understand that their position may not be needed for more than a few months, and they aren't expecting a career out of the work you give them.

If your freelancers are no longer needed, they will not take it to heart if you cancel the contract. Freelancers will do what they do best: find more work for their skills.

Common Reasons for Using Freelancers

- Your project is short term.
- You're working with a fixed budget.
- You want to leverage skills that may be more affordable and available outside your region or country.

- You're looking to expand your business with different levels of talent.

If you move to a fully remote operation with freelancers and ditch the expensive office, think about all of the other potential benefits you'll discover. Hiring freelancers can help you get your products to market earlier and increase your company's profitability in many ways. Some examples, depending upon your circumstances, include:

- Not needing a business building or office space — this means considerable savings in depreciation costs, lease expenses, or land purchases

- Not having to pay utility bills for those facilities — think about how the costs for electricity, water, sewage, phone service, heating, and related expenses can really add up

- No longer needing insurance for a building, equipment, and employees — but do check with your advisor regarding insurance-related issues

19

- Reduced maintenance or housekeeping expenses if you don't require a facility

- Not having to purchase office supplies, equipment, and certain other necessities for employees

- Freelance talent with specific skill sets based on your immediate requirements can provide faster results with a higher level of efficiency than trying to train an in-house person who doesn't have those unique skill sets.

Freelancers Versus Big Agencies

Why not just outsource tasks to a dedicated agency? Well, think of all the overhead the agency must cover. Also, you're giving away control. **The most compelling reasons to hire an individual rather than an agency are cost, expertise/experience, and having a more personal working relationship, resulting in a higher level of accountability.**

When you hire an individual, you only have to pay for that one individual and their services. You're not paying for an office, for less-experienced workers, and so on. Instead, you're paying for one person, who is extensively qualified to work with you. This is almost always cheaper than hiring an entire agency. (However, there are times when an agency can provide additional value if you need to leverage the agency's contacts or scale well beyond the ability of an individual freelancer).

When you hire an individual freelancer, you can also control the level of expertise/experience you're getting for your money. With some large agencies, people less qualified or less experienced end up doing the work for you, even though you are paying for the agency's top players. With a freelancer, you know exactly who you are working with on a project when you work directly with an individual.

This brings me to my next point. You get to develop a more personal working relationship with a freelancer because you are working directly with them, not with managers and supervisors. The freelancer also typically feels a greater responsibility to the project because it is a direct reflection on their work. This leads to higher accountability when things go wrong or problems need to be solved. It also means that you only need to communicate with one person, which can be less confusing than working with various layers of staff in a large agency.

Jim, who was developing an online company that offered business coaching courses and related training materials, wanted to get more visibility. He needed a writer to develop web content, someone to create a website, and someone else to periodically develop press releases high-lighting upcoming webinars or in-person speaking engagements.

Jim had worked with full-scale media agencies as an employee before he started his own business. He did the math. Agen-cies were expensive. Some of the larger ones shipped off pieces of a project to lower-skilled people, with a different per-son handling each phase. Each time Jim needed help with one aspect of production, he was transferred to the next person as-signed to take over. The lack of continuity was frustrating and time-consuming.

He also remembered having countless meetings with his former employer's mar-keting agency and paying significant fees to get communications developed. That worked for a company with a large budget. However, Jim no longer needed this pricey type of support. He just wanted someone who understood his objectives and was able to find the most cost-effective means to reach his marketing goals.

Jim found a highly experienced freelancer who helped him develop and implement communications strategies. She learned about his market and then wrote and distributed press releases and other announcements. Jim's costs were much less than what he would have paid an agency. He used this freelancer for ongoing projects and achieved excellent results.

Establish Two-Way Trust

Deciding to use a freelancer all comes down to trust. Business owners need to have confidence that the freelancer will accomplish their assignment. Freelancers, on the other hand, need to know that their client will be responsive to their questions, provide appropriate guidance, and pay on time.

Hiring freelancers is something I do every single day. Does this make me an expert in hiring the best freelancers? Well, not necessarily. But I can share some useful tips.

I don't allow myself to be overwhelmed and blinded by shiny reviews and out-of-this-world portfolios. They're sometimes too good to be true (or real). I also try to be fair and respectful. One freelancer can perform miracles for one client, but turn out to be mediocre with another. There are so many factors and circumstances to be taken into consideration. So, I want to see for myself whether a freelancer of my choice is the real deal.

I can be emotional. But that doesn't mean that I forget to be fair. Sometimes, there's no chemistry between me and a freelancer. This is nobody's fault. It just isn't working for us. There's no need to take or make it personal. I accept that I may not be a perfect match when it comes to my free-lancer's expectations. At the same time, I expect that my freelancer accepts my decision not to proceed with our work.

The freelancing process requires a delicate balance. I don't like to work with freelancers who just nod and repeat "Yes, Sir" automatically. At the same time, I can't work with freelancers who treat themselves as divas. I would rather work with a professional and reliable freelancer with the skill set and experience just a bit above average than with a freelance rock star who has a sense of entitlement. I tend to ask a lot of my freelancers, but I also like to give a lot in return. I believe in win-win scenarios.

I also try to build in enough time for improvisations. I want my freelancers to feel perfectly safe while working with me. On the other hand, I want to explore the possibilities and limits of our cooperation. In terms of fairness, I treat all freelancers the same. However, when it comes to hiring and working processes, every freelancer works differently.

chapter 2

Hiring and Managing a World-Class Team

What made me decide to leave my job and become a full-time professional freelancer before I started my own business? Well, the moment my freelance earnings matched my salary, I knew I was ready to make the leap. Being a full-time freelancer sounds great, but you must make sure that what you get in return is enough to support your current lifestyle—and going full-time means that freelancing becomes your primary source of income.

Making the Leap

As a traditional business owner, the concept of hiring freelancers through the Internet can seem like a daunting, if not scary, commitment to make. It's a leap from choosing someone based on the recommendation of a friend or neighbor. Personal recommendations sometimes work but limit your options.

> *If a friend recommends Laurie for a web design project, Laurie might say that she's busy for the next month, and you can't wait. You need someone available now. Also, while Laurie may have done a good job for your friend, her experience might be less relevant to your specific needs than the skills available from a wide range of online freelancers.*

When you hire someone from a freelance marketplace, you should be able to get a 360-degree view of the worker. That's one of the reasons why it's essential to choose an online freelance marketplace that has a transparent community built on creating value for businesses and freelancers.

- You need to be able to ascertain for yourself that a freelancer is qualified for your job.

- You need the capability to search for freelancers who haven't applied directly for your position if their credentials meet your needs.

- You should have the ability to interview applicants through various communication channels as well. That's why the online marketplace you choose should offer you the best talent with the highest digital reputations, where you can see their profiles, how they were rated, and samples of their work.

FAQs About Hiring Freelancers

Here are some of the top concerns people have when hiring freelancers:

How do I know that they will perform well? It's important to read reviews about their work, look at some of their projects, and carefully evaluate their experience. Make sure their skills are aligned with your objectives.

Start by clearly communicating the idea behind your project and describe your expectations. Use any available aids to prepare your freelancer for the project. For example, send photos, sketches, or even submit favorable work from other writers, programmers, or artists to give them an example of what you're expecting. The freelance world is based on creativity and input. You provide the input, and your freelancer will provide the creativity.

How do I know I'm not being scammed?

No one wants to be hurt financially, especially when trying something new. So, use a desktop application for all contracts that takes screenshots of the freelancer's desktop as this person is working. The app should function like a meter and should be able to report a productivity percentage in a work journal, which you can also review.

Any work produced while the app is running becomes billable and is subject to a five-day review period before payments are processed. Any discrepancies can be addressed before the freelancer is paid.

Will overseas freelancers speak English?

Many freelance sites work with talent around the world. Most of their freelancers possess an impressive level of English language skills, appropriate to their role. Copywriters and blog writers, for example, tend to know more about grammar and vocabulary than programmers. What we're finding is that communication is not the barrier it once was.

How about a freelancer's work ethic?

Rest assured, freelancers work as diligently as their full-time counterparts in traditional work environments, if not even harder. That's because they are marketing their unique skill sets, which may include diverse capabilities. Traditional employees may train for specific roles, jobs, or projects. The freelancer, however, trains to gain an advantage in the market with the goal of becoming highly employable. Plus, the harder they work, the faster they get paid and can move on to the next project.

What costs are associated with hiring freelancers? That depends on the platform you use. I don't think clients should have to pay a fee for hiring talent through an online marketplace. I think you should pay the freelancer's hourly rate, and that's it. Other companies may charge a flat rate or a percentage of the total. Be sure to research the details before you get started.

Can I vet the freelancer? You should always check out freelancers before hiring them, even through a trustworthy marketplace. First, look at their profile. See how much time and energy they have invested in creating a professional portfolio. This will give you an idea of the care and attention to detail they will bring to your project.

31

Next, make sure you're dealing with a real person. Despite privacy concerns, a good freelancer will go through verification steps with no hesitation. A picture is worth a thousand words, and a freelancer's profile picture is worth a thousand clients. Of course, freelancing isn't a beauty contest. But seeing that your potential worker is a real person is always reassuring.

Also, check out their digital credibility by verifying their identity on a variety of social media platforms. This includes having third-party links attached to their profiles on Facebook, Quora, Twitter, LinkedIn, and similar accounts.

The portfolio is very important. A candidate's online profile should detail work history, rates, reviews from previous employers, a summary of skill sets, and social links. Look over past projects, and see if some are similar to your own. However, don't allow yourself to be impressed to the point of complete blindness.

Instead, put the freelancer's skills to the test before hiring. Give that person a small (paid) assignment. This will help determine whether they actually wrote, designed, programmed, or otherwise created what's in the portfolio, and it will also give you an idea of their speed, accuracy, and attitude.

Finally, listen to your gut. If something looks fishy, it probably is. And if a freelancer's main draw is just a low price, that person is probably not worth your time and money.

Verifying the Freelancer

Once you have identified several promising candidates, do your homework to be sure that the person is verified.

- **Look at the number of reviews.** It's great to be able to work with a freelancer who has an inordinate number of five-star reviews. However, sometimes too many reviews are just too many. What's the ratio of the review numbers and the value of the projects? Do any reviews talk about repeat assignments?

- **Check whether your freelancer is verified.** There should be some "badges" or other information that list the skills attached to your freelancer's profile. All good platforms will ensure that their freelancers

33

have gone through a verification process. Freelancers should get the appropriate badges in return. If you don't have enough information, contact the provider's customer support team and ask them to confirm your potential freelancer's identity and credentials.

- **Review the portfolio items.** Fraudsters won't hesitate to present someone else's work as their own. So be careful, and do your homework. Some potential freelancers may insist that you protect their privacy and not contact previous clients. But you can still usually verify items in the portfolio.

- **Look for red flags.** Let's say your preferred freelancer is from another country and has an unbelievable amount of rave reviews. However, they're all from his own country and repeat the same praises over and over. Or you may spot questionable grammar mistakes. While the worker could be legitimate, I've heard rumors about freelancers "helping" each other by switching the roles of clients and freelancers to boost reviews. It would be helpful for a freelancer to have

reviews from all over the world and prefer-
ably a few from your country.

Special Tips for Startups

When you're the boss of a startup, you are the
only one who knows what you need, when you
need it, and who you need to make it happen.
Here are two points to keep in mind when bring-
ing in outsourced talent: ownership and recognizing the differences in various freelance positions.

Promote a sense of ownership. If you hire
freelancers and intend to use them to build your
business (as opposed to just completing a simple
task), then you will need to consider how you can
give them a sense of ownership. I don't think
ownership is that important with project-based
jobs. However, if you hire a project manager,
salesperson, social media manager, or other similar positions, then you will want them to feel invested.

Having a culture that nurtures relationships and
makes your people feel connected when they
work remotely can make all the difference. I'll discuss this in more detail in the following chapters.

Recognize the difference in various free-lance positions. If you're running a start-up, you'll want a few of your freelancers to feel more like real team members, even though they are technically temporary. However, you are most likely choosing to work exclusively with freelancers to keep costs low. So, you need to choose who you will work with on a regular, ongoing basis and who you can hire for one-off projects. Then structure your hiring accordingly.

Start on the Right Foot

If you want to attract and keep good people, you need to treat them well. Sometimes start-up owners have so much to do that they burn out their team. Or they may inadvertently replace good freelancers with less effective ones.

Establish clear communications from the outset.

- Describe the scope of the work.

- Be clear about deadlines.

- Make yourself available for conversations, and encourage questions.

- Communicate your brand values to free-lancers. Give them a copy of your mission statement. Make sure that they understand your brand, and are aligned with it.

Create a mission statement. Write several simple sentences that explain what you and your company value. This will be unique to your business. Here are a few samples:

- *We are passionate about making sure clients are thrilled with our services. We deliver on time every time.*

- *We accept feedback to improve the quality we deliver to our customers. We depend on each other, and each of us is dependable.*

- *We share ideas and mistakes openly. We communicate about potential problems, and we help each other improve the overall quality of our services.*

Choose a flexible platform to manage and pay workers. The platform you use should let you manage your team, track hours, find talent from around the world, and enjoy some peace of mind that jobs are being processed through a secure network.

Research a variety of freelance marketplaces to see which one suits your needs. Some sites charge fees. Others have an overload of talent. Some sites are user-friendly, and some are not. There are plenty of options available. I recommend a community-driven platform, where new features are installed because of community requests.

Get to know freelancers before hiring them. Talk with them on Skype. Learn about them. See what makes them tick. Ask questions about their portfolio, and be prepared to answer their questions about your business. Communication is everything.

Funding Options

Lack of funding shouldn't prevent your project from getting off the ground. In fact, most entrepreneurs struggle with capital and cash flow at some point. Don't let money issues slow you down from making your dream a reality.

You might want to consider a credit resource provided by your freelance marketplace. It can fund your project so that you can focus on running your business. It can be better than a bank loan because the approval process may be easier and faster. Freelance marketplaces that make this available can help give you a competitive advantage.

Common Misunderstandings

The most valuable currency in freelancing is trust. And the biggest problem for both the freelancer and client is to make sure they're working with real and credible individuals or companies. I've already talked about ways you can evaluate potential talent.

To flip the tables, let's look at questions that freelancers will be asking themselves about YOU:

Is the client legitimate? When bidding on a project, a freelancer should be able to tell whether their client's payment, email, phone number, etc., is verified. They also need to check that their client's profile is complete. You, as the client, should put as much effort and time into creating a profile as the freelancer. You should also make sure that all project details are accurate before posting.

Are there any suspicious links in a project's description? Communication, work, and payments outside the website are strongly discouraged and usually forbidden on all major freelance platforms. This is the only way that the platform can maintain quality control. If a client wants to provide details about the project in question, that's okay. The project descriptions should be thoroughly checked, and all clients should follow the proper way to use links in their project's descriptions.

Identify Preferred Platforms

Here's what to expect from an ideal platform when you're searching for freelancers:

Service fees are acceptable to both you and your freelancers. Many clients like to say, *"Why should I care? I don't pay freelance fees."* However, you do. Freelancers have to include fees into their final price in order to make a living. If you ask me, a service fee above 10% should make you raise your eyebrows.

Are you going to just spend your money, or will you be able to save some money for a change? I believe that the best freelance platform should reward and motivate businesses to spend more by hiring more freelancers or keeping them on for long-term projects. How? I'm talking about having some kind of cash-back option. The more you spend, the more you should be able to save.

Ensuring the digital credibility of your freelancer should be your right, not a privilege. You shouldn't waste your time trying to figure out whether a freelancer you want to hire is worth your trust. The best freelance platform shouldn't have anything against third-party links associated with their freelancers' account.

As mentioned earlier, you should be able to check your freelancer's Facebook, Twitter, LinkedIn, Quora, and similar accounts. Unfortunately, some platforms, by default, don't allow links to these accounts. Perhaps they're afraid you will take the work outside the platform itself and pay a freelancer directly. This is a narrow-minded approach, which hasn't proved to be particularly effective.

Having access to third-party platforms helps you do some screening in advance to get an idea of the freelancer's personality. Understandably, you want to know more about the freelancers you hire. Freelancers appreciate this feature, too,

41

because linking to other sites can get them suspended on some platforms.

A time-tracking tool should give you a quick and reliable overview. This is one of those things we take for granted. This tool should be more than just another basic app. Among other things, you should have a reliable indication of your freelancer's activity percentage, measured by their number of keystrokes and computer mouse movements. If you're happy with the deliverables and the activity percentage, there's no need to go any deeper into evaluating your freelancer's work.

Pricing should be fair for all parties. I encourage freelancers to ask for a fair rate that makes them happy and keeps them motivated to deliver quality work. After all, they have to earn enough to stay in business themselves.

I also advise our clients not to go after the lowest possible price. When you hire a freelancer at a very low price, you will likely eventually have to pay twice for the same work. Why? Well, you'll usually get lower-quality work. Then you have to pay some other freelancer to fix it. All of these costs and delays could have been easily avoided by focusing on quality first, and then price.

What to Ask in an Interview

An interview is the best way to draw distinctions between freelancers after you've reviewed their work. Here are some questions to ask that will help you decide which freelancer is the best fit for your requirements:

Are you able to meet the deadline for this project? Can you stick to the timeline? When you hire a freelancer, you are hiring someone who works on an as-needed basis for several clients. It is unlikely that you will be the freelancer's only client, and it is wise to make sure that the freelancer has enough time for your project. If the freelancer wavers while answering or is unable to commit to the timeline, you may want to look elsewhere.

With that said, you may find that top-tier freelancers are booked several months in advance. If your deadline can be extended or is not written in stone, consider these freelancers if you want a superior product. This is especially true if you need freelancers with more than a decade of experience.

43

What skills do you possess that are most relevant to this project? This is an excellent question because it allows freelancers to share their most valuable skills in relation to the scope of your project. Freelancers should be able to describe how they can help you and your project succeed.

Also, this question allows you to differentiate between candidates and to see whether the freelancer understands what you need in the project. In some cases, you may even learn about new skills that you didn't know the freelancer possessed. Ask freelancers to describe their skills and to detail why they could be useful throughout the project.

What do people like most about working with you? This is a fun question because it can throw freelancers for a loop and make them really *think* about what to say. The way that other people describe you says a lot about you. Most freelancers will have an idea of what people would say about them based on their self-awareness of their behavior at work.

If you can, call or email the freelancer's list of references to see if what they say about the freelancer matches up with the freelancer's response to this question. If the answers from the references don't align, this could be a red flag. It's worth investigating further before you decide.

If you are awarded this project, what will you do on the first day of work? This question may not always be appropriate, particularly if you haven't laid out the details or scope of work in the job description. However, it often allows you to look at the way that the person approaches work. It will give you a glimpse into the freelancer's time management and organizational skills.

Make sure that you also pay attention to whether the freelancer's plans correlate with what you have already shared about the project. For example, if you mentioned the need to first interview a subject matter expert before beginning work on the writing aspect of a project, then the freelancer should also understand this requirement.

What do you think is most important in a successful remote partnership? People work differently, and projects work best when people agree on a working style. Make sure that a freelancer shares your expectations about working remotely and supports your choice of communication style, whether it's email, text, Skype, chat, Google Hangouts, or phone calls—or a combination. The freelancer should know if you require weekly status updates, and what types of information should be included in communications.

Another part of this question can involve discussing the various tools for the project. If you use Todoist for project to-do lists, but your freelancer uses Evernote, then you will need to come to an agreement on which platform to use if your project involves shared lists. If your project requires extensive use of Hootsuite or Omnifocus, then you will most likely want a freelancer who has extensive experience using those apps or platforms. If an individual is not familiar with a particular app but has other essential skills, consider offering some training.

What is your experience in our industry?

While you may very well be willing to hire someone new to your industry, choosing someone with experience can often make your outsourcing experience run smoother. Follow up with specific questions about the freelancer's experience that relate to your project theme and concept. Look for ways in which the freelancer has approached similar tasks in the past.

Can you provide references? All high-quality freelancers who have worked for over a year should be able to provide you with at least one reference. Getting references can offer reassurance that the freelancer is a worthwhile investment. If you do contact the freelancer's references, you can also ask questions about what it was like to work with them. This will offer yet another perspective on whether the freelancer is a good fit for your project and working style.

How do you charge clients? What is included in your price? These are necessary questions because freelancers charge differently and utilize different pricing structures. You need to know whether revisions or changes to the project will require additional payments on a fixed-price job. You also need to be aware of how hourly pricing will work if the job is going to be billed on an hourly basis. Discussing approximate costs for projects and expectations on pricing from both sides can lead to a more harmonious working relationship.

Out of all the projects that you have worked on, which are you most proud of? Why were you proud of this project? Pay attention to what the freelancer liked about the project and the style of working. If you can mimic the working environment and add the same sensibility or creativity to your project, then you are more likely to receive the freelancer's best work and help that person excel.

Then follow up by asking what he or she might have changed if given more time or the opportunity to revisit the project. This often elicits really interesting comments, and you might learn something useful for your project.

Do you have any questions about the project? You should always ask this at the end of the interview. Don't be alarmed if there are no questions. If you do an excellent job of explaining the scope of the project or state that details will be shared after the hiring decision has been made, then don't expect any questions. At the same time, if a freelancer asks a pertinent question that's interesting and shows thoughtful consideration of the parameters, it's a good sign.

Remember to add a few of your own questions and personalize the interview process. Be as thorough as possible, and you will find the freelancer who is the perfect fit for your project.

Non-disclosure Agreements (NDAs)

After you've selected a freelancer, have that person sign an NDA. This should be a given. If you have an idea for a site and do not get your freelance web designer/developer to sign an NDA, this individual could walk away with your idea. You'll be discussing intricate details of your business with this freelancer, and you need to ensure that your freelancer keeps them confidential. Any freelancer who balks at an NDA should not be hired. You can easily create an NDA at sites/apps such as Rocket Lawyer or Shake.

chapter 3

Managing Diverse Skill Sets

People with diverse skill sets may need to be managed differently based on the type of work they do. Some may work more efficiently primarily with email communications, and others may require more frequent team meetings.

Set Realistic Expectations

All too often, clients and freelancers have different expectations about a project. For example, clients sometimes hire freelance designers and web developers to build an entirely new website for a very low rate and then feel slighted when the site is little more than a basic template. You usually get what you pay for. Know what you want done, estimate what that will realistically cost, and then build that into your budget.

Setting realistic expectations also includes thinking of a realistic timeframe for completing the project. Pushing freelancers too quickly can result in rushed, incomplete work. On the other hand, allowing freelancers as much time as they want often results in late projects or projects completed at the last minute. So, check in on their work to ensure that you are both satisfied with how things are progressing.

If you're hiring a writer based on an hourly rate, you and the writer should agree in advance the approximate cost for specific assignments. In some cases, this might involve a flat rate per project or a range. A range is often a good idea when you suspect that there might be scope changes ahead or even a change in project direction.

> *Nadia asked Raul to develop a customer success story for her website. She budgeted six hours, which included research, one customer interview, a first draft, and then a second draft plus additional minor revisions to it. After Nadia reviewed the story, she decided that Raul needed to interview two more people. Because the scope of the project had changed after it was assigned, Nadia needed to adjust the budget. It would have been unrealistic to expect Raul to undertake extra work and stay within the original budget.*

Having realistic expectations based on time and budget requirements is particularly important when you're dealing with software developers. Expectations must be clearly defined and easy to understand. After all, developers may strive for perfection. If you don't set clear boundaries about what to expect from a feature that's under development, you may experience "scope creep," which can be costly and delay the delivery of your company's products and services to customers.

Sean, a freelance software developer, was excited to create a new shopping cart for his client's products. The client, Maria, wanted a cart that provided very basic functions and required just enough data about the customer to process the transactions—address, name, credit card number, etc. But she failed to spell out the requirements in detail.

Sean, however, thought it would be valuable to get additional information about where the customer found out about the product, whether the customer wants to buy similar products and other extra details. While Sean was very proud of his work, it took longer than Maria expected. In addition, Sean had to remove some of

53

> *the features he designed because Maria*
> *wanted to limit the number of questions a*
> *customer had to answer before completing*
> *the transaction. If people have to fill in too*
> *much detail, they might decide it wasn't*
> *worth the effort, and take their business*
> *elsewhere.*

Be especially careful about making sure that the freelancer understands what's expected when working with people from other cultures. Don't make assumptions. The freelancer must be able to fully understand your needs and priorities. Communication matters. Timely communication is even better.

If you are working with freelance customer call center reps, give them scripts with extensive Q&As so that their answers are consistent with company policy, and issues don't have to be escalated. Whenever your policies are revised, send them updated scripts and provide training if needed.

Be Available, Timely, and Responsive

When you're busy managing your business, it's easy to brush aside questions from freelancers.

You might think you have more pressing matters to address. Keep in mind, however, that in order to meet your deadline, the freelancer might need your input. Without your feedback, your project could be delayed.

There's nothing more frustrating to freelancers than getting no response to a critical inquiry, especially after sending several emails trying to reach you. If you're busy when you're contacted, respond right away, saying you'll get back to them later. Or, put them in touch with someone else who can help them. Freelancers of all different skill sets need to feel valued. That's why it's essential to connect with them regularly and be responsive.

In some cases, all you might need to do is give freelancers the authority to decide on their own. Project managers and team leads, for example, should know when to check in with you, and when to move forward on their own. Another way to address this issue is to ask the freelancer to send you a brief email (one or two paragraphs) once a week that summarizes key accomplishments for the week and any areas where the freelancer needs help. This type of communication might work well with a software developer, web designer, writer, web developer, IT administrator, project manager, or team lead, for example.

In upcoming chapters, we'll look in more detail at various ways you can help remote workers feel more connected through virtual meetings, conference calls, emails, recognition programs, and other activities.

chapter 4

Creating a Great Culture in a Virtual World

Countless articles and business management books have been written about the importance of having an effective corporate culture. The culture of your workplace influences productivity, retention, recruitment, and even your company's profitability and innovation. However, some of the most exciting businesses don't have a workspace at all. Instead, 21st-century organizations, like digital agencies, e-commerce companies, and consultants, have remote teams located all over the globe. Often, only a handful of team members are online at any given time. So, how does that impact the need for having a remote culture?

Culture Matters

Having a well-understood culture based on your corporate vision and commitment to customers and freelancers may be even more important for remote teams than those who are working with everyone on the same campus. A great company culture provides team members a shortcut for making the kind of decisions that move a company forward. When you have people spread out across several time zones, it can be harder to get answers to time-sensitive questions. You can't simply walk down the hall to find a resolution. Your team members may not even be awake when you are working.

If your team members all understand and follow the company culture guidelines, they will know what to do in various circumstances. For example, if a customer has a complaint, your culture might be based on doing whatever it takes to make that customer satisfied.

Besides, having a strong, positive culture gives your team a sense of community. After all, remote freelancers can often get lonely, since they spend most of their time in front of a computer screen. A well-communicated and effective company culture helps team members feel as if they are part of something bigger than themselves, instead of just being a hired hand.

When people feel connected to a larger mission, their productivity improves. They are less likely to leave for another opportunity. When your remote team shares common values, they are also more likely to speak up when they find a mistake or propose a good idea. If the freelancers get rewarded for out-of-the-box recommendations that drive business, that's even better.

What makes a culture great? It is a combination of many elements:

- Having core values and a clear mission
- Encouraging collaboration
- Recognizing and celebrating success
- Following effective processes and goals
- Creating a sense of community
- Encouraging respect and trust
- Focusing on innovation and excellence
- Having a passion and pride in work
- Being willing to take risks
- Demonstrating powerful, positive leadership
- Providing open communication

Culture by Choice or Circumstance?

The truth about your company culture is that it already exists. You can promote a particular culture intentionally, or it will develop as a result of circumstances. Too often, founders of remote companies might neglect the idea of focusing on their culture, which unintentionally creates an environment that instills procrastination, is based on just being "good enough," and is obsessed with just completing more transactions.

Team members are less likely to collaborate under these circumstances. The work may begin to suffer, and even extremely talented team members might eventually turn in work of a steadily declining quality. If all that's demanded of them is to do something that's just passable, then that's what they'll do.

If this is not the type of team you want working in your business, you must promote the kind of company culture you do want to see. You have to structure interactions in a way that models your vision for success.

Write a mission statement and a well-articulated plan to build a productive culture for team members. There are so many different pieces of a puzzle to take into consideration. With remote teams, you have to develop an environment that will unite your workers. They will think of themselves as a powerful team, even though they may be thousands of miles away from each other. Keep in mind that the majority of remote teams never meet face-to-face.

How are you supposed to come up with a win-win scenario in this situation? It all goes back to having a shared mission and a culture that focuses on supporting the needs of our freelancers and clients. I'll discuss more about developing a mission statement in the next chapter.

Why You Need a Suitable Culture Fit

As previously mentioned, according to industry research, we are likely to witness the absolute domination of remote-working teams over traditionally fixed-office teams by 2025. The pandemic in 2020 led companies to realize just how many jobs could be done remotely that hadn't been previously considered.

When it comes to successful and productive organizations, the culture—corporate values and processes that support those values — has become more critical than ever. The distributed teams just can't make it without a healthy environment where people feel acknowledged and supported.

So, what are the ways for remote workers to work as a team as if they have shared the same office space for years, every single day, around the clock? Here are some approaches to consider:

Thoughtful Hiring and Training

Have you ever used the wrong jigsaw piece? Then you know how it feels to hire the wrong employee for your team. Something just doesn't fit correctly. You may find a business rock star with immense potential. However, if this person isn't a perfect fit for your specific company culture, then that freelancer may not work out.

For example, the freelancer may be highly skilled but not want to engage in team communication or give other team members credit for their work. Perhaps this individual is a diva, and the other team members resent her. If you follow the requirements of your culture when you're hiring, and look for people who are problem solvers and collaborative, you can avoid this issue.

We all know how important it is to ensure proper training for new team members. Traditional teams have plenty of time to train new members. We can't say the same for remote teams. Time and opportunities to expose new members to cultural values and practices are precious, and resources tend to be limited in the remote business world. When you're working remotely, you can't just sit around and wait for new members to absorb the culture.

What's the solution for training remote workers? New workers should have enough time and training resources at their disposal. Let your cultural imagination run wild. Feel free to experiment. You can make videos where you describe your company's culture, and ask for feedback.

Some companies also create a short document that lists your corporate values. When you gather these resources, you'll have a useful library for future training that can ensure a more personal and impactful way to reach your freelancers.

I'd also like to stress the value of team leaders, which I refer to as "first-among-equals." A great team leader delegates the workload according to the capabilities of teammates. While they report to the team leader, the members have a certain amount of freedom to complete their jobs. More freedom equals more creativity. When team members have good working conditions and feel appreciated, they have more respect for the team leader's authority. Remote team members need to be comfortable with their team leader in order to discuss any problems they may face. That's why the first-among-equals management principle is an effective approach for a productive and transparent remote team culture.

Team Meetings and One-on-Ones

When you're spending time with your team in the same office, you can always find an opportunity to hold a meeting. But when they are scattered all over the world, you have no choice but to schedule remote team meetings to celebrate positive results. Remote managers shouldn't let these meetings turn into mere status updates. You need to create that special feeling that family members share when they sit down together to share a meal (assuming that they're a functional family, of course). All teammates should be able to catch up with the team's progress during these meetings. More importantly, they should be encouraged to speak freely about what's on their minds and in their hearts.

To maximize meeting efficiency, set up regular departmental gatherings as well as team and one-on-one sessions. The trick is to avoid having too many meetings, which stress out team members and can negatively affect performance. On the other hand, you need meetings to run your business successfully. That's why top management and team leaders should organize both small-team (individual) and "all-hands" meetings when all remote team members are present.

All-hands meetings shouldn't last too long if you have properly organized and executed individual and small team meetings. The safest bet is to have a big all-hands meeting once a month, and smaller departmental meetings once a week.

One-on-one meetings are important and shouldn't be reserved only for traditional teams. You can still achieve the desired level of intimacy and trust through individual video calls. If your remote worker needs help at an individual level, you can organize a special meeting just for that person. One-on-ones should become an integral part of your remote culture. Freelancers need to know that they can always count on fully individualized support. At the same time, meetings shouldn't be reserved only for your organizational vertical (management-freelancer) structure, but should also include an organizational horizontal structure among peers (freelancer-freelancer).

Two core freelancers on my team from different countries get together periodically just to brainstorm. They share ideas for existing activities and as well as what they might do in the future to innovate. They've established a powerful digital friendship, which I'll describe in more detail in Chapter 6.

Remote Appreciation Tips

One trouble with remote teams is that you can't have in-person, face-to-face ways to recognize the worker of the month. However, this doesn't mean that public recognition, even remotely, can't have a positive effect on your team. Whether you say it at a meeting, or share it through a chat or email, *"a job well done"* always sounds and feels good for teammates. Recognition has always been and still is one of the most effective ways to keep your team motivated.

Speaking highly of someone at the start of a meeting isn't the only way to reward remote team members. You might set up a virtual board where different members can thank each other for a job well done. You can reward team members with paid subscriptions for their favorite apps or tools. These don't necessarily have to be associated with work. Consider purchasing a subscription to a popular streaming service for a high-achieving remote team member, who would be very grateful to receive this gift. You can also recognize team members by giving them incentives, such as a gift card, a plaque for their home office, a company T-shirt, or other items.

You don't need to spend a fortune on state-of-the-art technology to strengthen your organizational culture. Remote freelancers are generally grateful for work and are not a very demanding group. Managing them requires just a little bit of your attention, and what you get in return is the solid foundation for your company to grow. With a thoughtful approach and attention focused on the practices I've shared, it won't matter if team members are located in different cities, countries, or continents.

The "goCulture" Approach

From the very beginning, our platform has been focused on solving the challenges of modern business and the freelance economy. We have learned, experimented, and developed features *with* our users. We refer to this tight relationship between our freelancers, teams, and clients as our goCulture, which has helped us become what we are today. We are willing to share this invaluable experience with the countless remote teams all over the world.

> One of our clients has freelancers in San Diego, Portland (Maine), and Serbia. They all work together and care deeply about each other's families. Even though they have never actually met in person, they know each other pretty well. It's both amazing and inspiring to witness how they stand up for each other and collaborate simultaneously on a daily basis.

> On Fridays, for example, they often have a beer together while they are in a video conference. That is the remote workforce goCulture they have been able to develop while working together on our platform. You don't have to meet in person to build

*trust and have friendly, professional rela-
tionships.*

Right Tools for the Right People

Without effective technology, remote teams
wouldn't be able to do their jobs. Thankfully,
there are many apps and software to help them.
For instance, the Trello app keeps you organized
with your work projects, tasks, and deadlines. A
very popular option for remote teams is to use
Slack as a virtual office. Having a virtual office
means people will be able to get immediate feedback about their work, as well as connect with
their coworkers.

Slack is software that's like a chat room for your
company. People use it to help teams collaborate
seamlessly on projects, and it reduces the need to
send many emails back and forth.

Regular team meetings aren't enough because they
only happen once every two weeks. If there's a
change of plans or a mistake that needs to be cor-
rected, teams have to be notified immediately.
That's why Slack is so helpful with communication.

- Team members can easily send larger files and get speedy feedback on their work.

- With Slack's specialized search, you can quickly find the product information.

- You can even check the status of current products in the sales cycle.

- In the end, Slack saves you time and enables you to spend more time on actual work.

A big challenge in managing a remote team is that you have to deal with different time zones. Luckily for remote workers, technology makes it easier to overcome this obstacle. For example, you can use Time Zone Buddy, an app that keeps track of all time zones, to schedule the most convenient meeting time for remote team members. Sometimes, even with this app, it is nearly impossible to have the perfect time for a meeting that will suit everyone.

Since there is always going to be somebody who will have to go to bed late or wake up early, just do your best to find a time that will be acceptable for the majority. You can't please everyone. There may even be times when you need to break up your meetings into two groups with two separate sessions based on time zones.

Remote Corporate Retreats

Unlike regular workplaces, remote team members don't have the chance to bond with their coworkers over mealtime. This makes corporate retreats even more critical for remote teams. Usually, corporate retreats are annual events. They represent an opportunity for remote team members to meet their client and coworkers in person, as well as do some work and do some team building. Nothing bonds people more than hiking, sports, or karaoke. Even if one or two people won't be able to make it, try and gather as many remote team members as possible when it's feasible to gather as a regional group.

If travel and related circumstances make this impossible, consider having a virtual retreat. Set aside a day when people will gather on Zoom, and plan it like an event. If you want to add a personal touch, consider sending corporate mugs or T-shirts to the participants in advance and order a food delivery service in their city to send them a meal at the end of the day. Food is a big motivator!

Here's a simple idea for strengthening and promoting both your brand and your remote culture. Your remote team members can wear T-shirts with your company's logo during meetings. They can choose to decorate the walls behind their workspace with company posters. Yes, we're talking about one kind of "product placement" that can be very beneficial for your team. How about giving your freelancers a coffee mug with your company's logo and placing it in front of the camera at the meetings?

In-Person Visits

Traveling around the world isn't the cheapest option, and may be very restrictive, if not prohibitive during the COVID-19 pandemic. However, going forward it may be necessary if you manage a remote team. Visiting your team members' cities and meeting face-to-face with them makes them feel appreciated. You will be able to meet their families as well, and see what drives them as individuals. Personal visits are proven to be a sure way to boost the morale and confidence of your remote team members, which will improve their work performance in return.

Write Your Own Rules

Every remote team culture needs its own rules because every team is different. What works for one team might not work for another. That's mainly because each remote team may have unique business plans, and the same rules don't always apply. Without proper team rules, the remote team won't be able to do its job efficiently.

To work effortlessly, the team leaders need to write their own team culture rules that team members will abide by. Here are some sample guidelines to develop an effective team culture:

- Treat team members with respect.

- Feel free to ask questions during a meeting, but wait until the presenter is finished.

- If you think you might have trouble meeting a deadline, notify your team lead right away.

- Send a brief status report to the team lead at least once a week.

- If you know when you'll be unavailable for work, let your team lead know right away.

- We encourage open communication.
  There's no such thing as a dumb question.

Test Your Culture

Often the founder is the last one to know how workers perceive the corporate culture. If you want to discover what your company culture is composed of right now, ask your team what they enjoy most about working with you.

Pay attention to see if their actions match up to their words. You will most likely be shocked at what you hear and see as you start to notice what your team members actually think. They may not see themselves as a team at all. Each person may think of themselves as an autonomous vendor or freelancer who happens to work for you.

If you want to change the company culture, you need to understand what it currently is like today and what you want it to be. When you have a remote team, you can't install ping-pong tables and vending machines to encourage informal gatherings. Instead, you have to find a way to bring people from a variety of different locations and backgrounds together to buy into the company culture that will best serve the business.

Here are seven steps you can take to build a business environment that will improve productivity, loyalty, and customer satisfaction.

1. Define your culture. You can't put anything in place unless you first understand what type of culture you want your remote team to have. The more specific you are in defining your culture, the more success you will have implementing it. The best place to start is with a list of values that are important to you. This will be specific to you and your business. Make the list as long as you want. Think about the values you consider to be the most important to instill as part of your business culture. Some values you may want to list include:

- Focus on customers.

- Welcome feedback.

- Communicate openly.

- Share ideas freely.

- Meet commitments.

When building a culture, you are really creating an operating system for your business. The culture will be what team members turn to when they need to make a business decision. You want this operating system to be simple. If it is too bloated, it won't work. The system will help employees make the right decisions, even when you are not available to answer questions or provide feedback.

2. Create a mission statement. The initial list of values is for your eyes only. Giving your remote team a list of 25 values will only annoy or confuse them. The basics of your business culture need to be simple so that they can easily become second nature.

Transform your personal values list into a brief mission statement. Don't panic. You don't need some massive three-page declaration of what your business is about. An ideal mission statement for remote teams will be one to three sentences long. (See the example of a mission statement in Chapter 2). The shorter, the better. That means you will have to narrow down your list of values to no more than five.

Your mission statement is not something written for customers or clients. It doesn't need to be on your website. However, it should be a part of your communication with your team. The more you share it and talk about it, the faster everyone will realize how important it is. Ask everyone to commit to the mission statement.

3. Evaluate team members based on the mission statement. Hold everyone accountable for following the principles you laid out. Depending on your style, this can be formal, informal, or a mix of both. If you hold regular reviews with your team members, make going over their compliance with the mission statement part of that process.

If you have an informal management style, mention the mission statement in regular communications. Praise a team member who spotted a mistake, even if it was outside of that person's area of responsibility. Thank a team member who communicated early on about needing a deadline extension. Remind team members of the importance of being dependable when they miss a deadline. The evaluation does not need to be harsh, but it does need to happen regularly with all team members if you want the new culture to take hold.

4. Have brief virtual meetings. People are social animals. We pick up on body language and tone of voice. Communicating strictly by email or instant message limits the amount of information you can share. Holding brief virtual meetings where everyone can at least hear each other, and ideally see each other, will help everyone feel like they are part of a common cause. It is easier to feel loyalty and empathy with people that you have seen and talked to. Meetings do not need to be long. Use even brief meetings to reiterate the values in your mission statement.

> *Javier, who owned an online cosmetic business, had a team of call center freelancers located in the Philippines. The group had been together for about two weeks. All communications were done via email, Slack, and chats. The reps were highly skilled, dedicated workers, but they needed an online, face-to-face meeting to feel more connected with the business and work more effectively with customers.*

> *It wasn't until Javier called an all-hands meeting on Zoom and discussed the mission statement, the importance of their roles, the company culture, and other topics that the reps felt confident and*

comfortable in their roles. They quickly became happier and more productive.

5. Have your best team members recruit others. When you need to add to your team, ask your top performers to help recruit people. Chances are they know people in their networks who are just like them. The recruits will naturally look to the person who brought them in for clues on how to act as part of the organization. Having your team members be your recruiters will help strengthen your organization.

6. Deal with dissenters. Despite your best efforts, it's possible that not all team members will buy into your culture. If you've explained the importance of your company's values and how it's part of the corporate culture, and some people object to it, ask them why. If their reasons aren't valid, consider removing these members from your team. Allowing doubters to spread baseless objections can undermine your authority and have a negative impact on the team. Letting people go is never fun, but it is sometimes essential for running a vibrant business that is built to outlast you.

7. Have team members evaluate you.

One of the best ways to prove that you take your culture seriously is to make sure you model the values you teach. But it can be challenging to see our own inconsistencies. So, ask team members to hold you accountable for following the mission statement. This shows them that you are committed to walking the talk and that you aren't asking them for anything you are not willing to do yourself. When you let your team evaluate your performance, you are also allowing them to grow closer together.

chapter 5

Moving from Skype to Zoom to 3D Virtual Meetings

Unproductive meetings are to blame for billions of lost dollars every year. This is especially true when your business is entirely remote. Organizing a remote meeting means that you have a lot of prep work to do. These best practices and tools can help:

Remote Meeting Guidelines

Proper preparation is everything. When planning a remote meeting, don't forget to consider time zone differences. There are plenty of useful world clock apps. Only include remote team members who are essential! Also, make sure they have enough time to review materials and prepare for the meeting. If you plan to use a specific communication tool or software, check beforehand to determine that all participants have it and know how to use it.

Follow established protocol. Explain and enforce standard remote meeting "etiquette":

- Keep the space behind you clean and professional.

- Look directly into your camera.

- Dress appropriately. Just because workers are remote, it doesn't mean they should attend a meeting in pajamas.

- Allow for a few seconds delay when asking or answering a question.

- Assign a moderator to keep discussions on point.

Practice in advance. Before you set a date and time for your remote meeting, discuss the software and communication tools that participants feel comfortable using. Ask attendees to test their gear before the meeting. The last thing you need is for someone to be left out because that person couldn't hear or see what was going on in the meeting.

Share screens. Sharing your screen during a remote meeting can be the most crucial part of the process, letting you illustrate new concepts, strategies, business plans, and other information. Again, you have to be careful in choosing the most suitable share screen solutions and contents that are acceptable for all team members.

Put participants in charge. You can't expect your meeting to be a success with only passive participants. That's why assigning responsibilities to remote meeting participants is always a good idea. For example, one team member could be a facilitator. Another can keep track of time. Have someone else take notes. If all remote team members have a role, then you'll have fewer problems following the agenda.

Focus on time management. In a remote meeting, every single second is precious — for both you and your participants. So, don't permit interruptions or diversions. Also, be sure to include everyone. Allow enough time for everybody to share their thoughts and contribute. Set aside time for Q&As.

Have a plan for starting and ending the meeting. Send an invitation and check that all participants are available. Then start and end your remote session on time. This helps build a culture of respect and efficiency. Before you complete a meeting, reiterate what every team member needs to know about future actions on both the corporate and individual level. About five or ten minutes before the meeting ends, briefly summarize what was covered and agreed upon. Follow up with an email, clarifying expectations for each team member.

Skype or Zoom?

If your freelancers don't want to use Skype, but Skype is your primary way of connecting, then it's time to lay down the law. You can download Skype on any software, including Windows, IOS, Android, Linux, and multiple web browsers. It lets you share files, use a whiteboard, share screens, conduct video calls, record meetings, and store files in its cloud. You can do a video call for an unlimited amount of time. The free version has its limits, so you should buy a business version. There are Microsoft Basic Business, Standard Business, and Office 365 E3 versions. When you buy a business plan, you also get access to Microsoft Teams.

Another popular tool is Zoom. This app is a better choice than Skype when you have more participants in the meeting. The free version limits your meeting time to 40 minutes and 100 participants. The premium version of Skype currently allows up to 250 participants.

Zoom, in comparison, has a plan that offers a capacity of 1,000 participants to attend at the same time. Skype charges you a monthly rate per participant, and Zoom charges you per host. On Zoom, you can create groups of participants, do a virtual hand raise, mute other peoples' mics, touch up your appearance, etc. You can even download the app on your phone. If you want any additional features, you'll have to pay a monthly sum. For example, if you're going to hold webinars, you'll have to pay extra.

The 3D Virtual World

I really enjoy putting on my Oculus Quest headset and entering virtual worlds— whether I'm out there killing zombies, playing ping pong, or competing in a cross-country race. A good friend of mine gave me the headset so that we could hang out periodically in the virtual world. He's also a customer, and while we're playing games, we can discuss business ideas. What I like about being in these worlds is that once you put on your headset, there are no distractions. You simply cannot leave the "room."

Over time I started to meet with other customers and advisors, along with my operations manager, using these headsets. Now I'm even wearing the headsets in virtual meeting rooms. My avatar is having meetings in these virtual reality environments with people. (You can appear in these meetings without an avatar, but that takes up more bandwidth and, besides, it's kind of fun having a cartoon-like version of myself in the "room.")

I plan to expand this and get more headsets at some point because these meetings are so much fun and are very productive. The technology forces me to avoid the distractions of checking emails, answering a text, or trying to multitask and search online while I'm having a meeting. Once you put on the headsets, you are really focused. We can even all look at the same documents together that are projected in the virtual meeting room.

The world is becoming more virtual by the day. We are lucky to be working at a time where we can experience the benefits of meeting together in the same place without leaving our home. It's fun and exciting. I can't wait to see what's next.

Dynamic Written Collaboration

Collaborative tools like Slack, Basecamp, Google Docs, and Trello all have the option of integrating with other apps. Without them, freelancers might have to write 100 emails daily. The chat layout of these apps eases the process of searching for information. If you had to communicate with your team members via emails, you'd have to read each email to find the information you need. Communication and management apps have search options that enable you to quickly find what you need. You can even make video and audio calls with them.

The best part of using these collaborative tools is that you don't have to get out of the app to send files, text messages, ask for instructions, etc. Google Docs is a cheaper option that enables you to share any file types in your chats. Although Trello mainly focuses on project organization, freelancers use it for communication as well.

Basecamp is an alternative to Trello. When using any of these apps, pay attention to third-party conversation topics, which files you are sharing in which chat, and who is an admin.

chapter 6

Building a Loyal Freelance Workforce

People need to feel appreciated and valued. I've known many remote workers who left corporate jobs because they felt left out. Their emails and phone calls often weren't answered. They didn't get invited to team meetings where their input would've been valuable. No one ever asked them how they were doing personally. They didn't have insight into the big-picture vision that clients or employers wanted them to achieve. They were lonely, and after long periods of failing to get recognition for their accomplishments or even be listened to, they simply left. That's how to destroy loyalty.

When you're working with remote talent, you need to find a variety of ways to help them feel part of your team. That's essential for driving productivity and innovation. I can't emphasize enough the power of meeting directly with people, and how it impacts your workforce and results. Of course, your meetings have to be meaningful and informative.

Try to maintain a balance between work and casual time in meetings. You can't spend the whole session talking only about work. So, CEOs should kick off virtual meetings with chats about topics that aren't work-related. A couple of minutes spent talking about sports, movies, or kids relaxes everyone. If they're relaxed, the meeting will go faster and be more productive. Small talk also makes freelancers more connected to you, which can generate loyalty.

Praise is very important, too. When your team is doing a great job, give credit where it's due. Don't forget to acknowledge the hard work and success of freelancers during a meeting. The freelancers that you praised will work harder and produce even better results. Even the rest of the team members will be motivated to do a better job, just so they can be praised in the next meeting.

The Power of Digital Friendships

Encourage digital friendships. This is the secret ingredient every productive remote team culture needs. But how do you help nurture them?

A remote manager encouraged Susan, a freelance writer from the United States, to have weekly meetings with her graphics designer, Leena, located in Europe. Over time, they became good friends and looked forward to their sessions. The quality of their work became more creative and effective. They were able to develop award-winning digital content that also helped their clients generate more leads and increase sales by 25% in just a few months.

Just because you know a couple of things about your remote team members, it's not enough to build sincere and long-lasting friendships in the digital world. You may set someone's birthday reminder, and feel good about it. But that's not enough to create a genuine relationship. In the best-case scenario, you will get a smiley icon in return. Digital friendship as a part of the remote team culture has to be built one important step at the time. So, what are the right steps to take with your workers?

Five Minutes Before (and After) Meetings

What are you doing while waiting for a remote meeting to begin? Are you checking your head-phones? Okay. Are you waiting for all remote team members to join a call? That's okay, too. You don't have to be silent. However, exchanging a few words can break the awkward silence and boost rapport. Ask some simple questions like, "How are you doing? Does anyone have an interesting story to share?"

Think about what's happening after you finish your remote meeting. It's better to end with some positive information so that people can look forward to the next meeting, instead of frantically waiting to get off the call.

Personalize Your Remote Visit

A remote colleague once used a web camera to show me his new state-of-the-art gaming chair. I returned a favor by adding my dog to our call. Isn't this something you would do with your friend from the "real" world?

During the before-or-after meeting chats, ask for movie or TV show recommendations. Look for something you can all discuss, even if it's the weather. Many global sporting or music events are impossible to ignore. The connections you make during so-called chit chat may turn out to be your key takeaways from the meeting.

Ten Ways to Increase Loyalty

1. Give clear guidance on what's expected.

2. Provide growth opportunities — creatively and financially.

3. Listen to concerns and respond.

4. Make everyone feel valued and appreciated.

5. Say thank you and mean it.

6. Show participants how their work fits into the overall corporate vision.

7. Pay fairly, quickly, and in the currency of the workers' choice.

8. Schedule periodic meetings and allow time for small talk.

9. Allow flexibility in schedules and deadlines.

10. Provide tools to help participants succeed — a time tracker, work diary and

monitoring system, and a flexible, versatile payment system.

chapter 7

Tackling Global
Currency Challenges

Many small businesses that rely heavily on remote, global online freelancers face a significant challenge in finding the most flexible and cost-effective ways to pay them. Dealing with currency exchanges can be expensive and time-consuming. Think about it.

If your businesses can't simplify the payment process while also complying with financial regulations worldwide, you're going to have unhappy freelancers.

That's why you need to find an efficient way to pay overseas talent. This will make it easier to recruit the best talent, whether it's people who do customer service, software development, web design, marketing, customer support, or other functions.

Think Like a Freelancer

Freelancers want to choose how they will be paid, and they must receive funds in a timely manner. This could be through a bank account, debit or credit card, payment advance, digital transfer, or even crypto. It might involve working with different currencies or multiple payment vendors. Some countries may only process certain types of payments.

The problem with payments is the fees, especially transaction and currency-changing fees. Visa and Mastercard are the most common credit cards in Eastern Europe. A few banks have American Express. If you use any other credit card, you'll most likely have to transfer the payment to the freelancer via PayPal. This means yet another fee that's cut into a freelancer's paycheck.

> *Dmitry, a freelancer, earns $200 on a project. But by the time he transfers the funds into his account, he has only $160 left. The payout period can be up to five days, not including weekends. Time zone differences between banks can delay it even further. So, a freelancer from Eastern Europe, like Dmitry, has to carefully plan which payment solution to use.*

In the Philippines, for example, traditional banking services to process cross-border payments could reach up to 7% and can be very slow. To reduce this cost while paying freelancers faster and securely, goLance leverages the blockchain technology and the digital asset XRP through Ripple's On-Demand Liquidity (ODL) product. This enables us to make hyper-efficient, low-cost payments that can happen in real-time, and it keeps our customers happy.

> *Angelo was a highly skilled call center operator in the Philippines. Although workers in that part of the world are paid considerably less than in the United States, the cost of living there is relatively low. He struggled with his former U.S.-based client because it took weeks from the time he worked until the time he was paid, and the currency exchange fees were high and unpredictable. When he switched to working through goLance, which leverages Ripple's ODL, it was like getting a good raise. Plus, he had the money in his hands immediately.*

As mentioned earlier, freelancers should have a meter and work diary to record their activity, track the time spent on an assignment, and communicate the project's status to clients. All of this needs to be integrated into the payment platform so that workers can receive timely electronic payments into their accounts.

Flexible Payment Options

Businesses that use global freelancers may require a variety of electronic payment options. Some platforms make this possible with low-cost exchange rates and pricing from numerous suppliers. This can be integrated with PayPal, Payoneer, Wyre, Transpay, Tipalti, Ripple, Currencycloud, AFEX, OFX, or others.

Because of these integrations, the platform you use can help automate the entire payment process. This can include providing money transfers and digital payments services and even offering bitcoin services quickly and securely. The result is that users can access real-time exchange rates and have fast, secure, convenient, and lower-cost international transfers. Businesses can scale and gain a competitive edge when they use a freelance marketplace that makes it easy to manage and pay freelance staff efficiently, flexibly, and cost-effectively.

chapter 8

Managing Remote Freelancers: Case Studies

All businesses must overcome a variety of obstacles. It's not the problems you face that will make the difference between success and failure or just getting by. Rather, it's how you react to those challenges. In some of the earlier chapters, we discussed best practices for managing a remote culture. Now let's look at additional real-life examples so you can see how to put these practices into play.

We'll explore some common examples related to managing remote freelancers. These include having the ability to:

- **Scale and pay quickly**: Being able to ramp up and bring in help for big projects without having to deal with administrative issues.

- **Manage remotely**: Switching from managing people in a physical office to supervising them offsite.

- **Tackle technical limitations**: Addressing issues related to bandwidth and connectivity.

- **Encourage teamwork and recognize accomplishments**: Building team loyalty and recognizing staff.

- **Connect and communicate**: Finding innovative ways to communicate.

- **Address cultural issues**: Sharing and executing a shared vision while considering cultural diversity.

Scale and Pay Quickly

One enterprising freelancer started his journey as a freelance software developer for a digital marketing business and was also helping to develop and test the initial website for a startup. Today, he's the proud owner of an agency that includes 12 remote technical workers in Warsaw and Eastern Europe. He attributes this success to his hard work, excellent team, and freelance platform, which helped to make his dream of owning a thriving agency a reality.

He has an incredible work ethic and thrives on the flexibility of doing business remotely as a freelancer and manager of an agency that does website development, systems administration, and coding for a variety of industries. He wanted to take on more clients to expand his business but needed to bring in other people in order to scale quickly. This required finding the best talent for his agency and using a comprehensive, flexible platform that would eliminate the tedious manual efforts involved in time tracking and billing.

As he used his platform to find more contractors to support his agency, he was able to ramp up business and increase his client base from supporting about three to five clients at a time to more than 65. The platform has enabled his business to flourish due to its fast, accurate, and easy payment system, which provides everything needed to do reporting and billing.

His platform's system tracks the time his contractors work and is integrated with payment processing. His contractors appreciate the opportunity to find work with low-cost fees, a reliable system, and fast payments.

Manage Remotely

A US-based consumer finance company needed to lower costs, increase productivity, and expand with a remote workforce. This growing company wanted to reduce the time and expense involved in managing an onsite call center for customer service and other functions. As the company moved more work from its in-house call center to remote staff, the business reduced costs but also needed additional technology to better manage remote workers.

The company's CEO was able to cut payroll costs in half and boost productivity with dedicated, tech-savvy remote workers. The screen reporting capability offered by his platform made it easier and much less expensive to manage remote workers than to track the work of people sitting in the company's office.

Because the platform provided extensive features that simplified managing workers remotely, the company was able to hire more remote workers to support further growth, while also reducing expenses. Contractors now log their daily work hours into a time tracker, which monitors their work through messaging, entries in a work diary, desktop screenshots, and activity reports. The platform lets managers check in on a worker's progress, gauge daily "on-the-job" productivity, and view an accurate record of billable work hours from their contractors.

An added bonus was that as more work shifted to a fully remote model, with just the managers remaining on-site, the business reduced the burden of maintaining onsite equipment for the operational team.

Tackle Technical Limitations

Dealing with people in different time zones is often a headache for freelancers. If you're lucky, your team will have at least a couple of freelancers in the same time zone. Video calls are only suitable for meetings. Updates and files usually must be sent over other means of communication, such as apps like Slack.

Teams shouldn't have to worry about choosing the perfect communication app for their team. They should have one integrated into the platform they use for projects. A good one should let you send files and messages securely without leaving the platform. Because it's already accessible, there's no need to take the extra step of downloading an app.

Teamwork and Morale

In previous chapters, we discussed the importance of team meetings and ways to give everyone an opportunity to contribute. Digital friendships are critical for helping teams to collaborate effectively. Finding unique ways to recognize some of your key players goes a long way to maintaining an innovative, dedicated culture. I'll cite some of my personal experiences as a case study.

When I started goLance, I attended a conference in Moscow. While there, I decided to take a side trip to Siberia to meet with a goLance freelancer who was a top performer. It was an arduous adventure, but I am passionate about the freelancers that support my team and wanted to personally thank him for his contributions. I visited his home and met his family. I got to see firsthand how his work made such a difference in his life. I know that he really appreciated me traveling so far to see him.

Sometimes just a simple thank-you email can boost morale. I make it a point to send out emails congratulating and recognizing people for their contributions. These emails go to everyone involved, and I explain why I value their contributions and what it means to the business.

It's so important to lead by example. If your key team knows that you're responsive and available when they need you, or within a reasonable time period, it gives them confidence that you're looking out for them and appreciate their efforts.

Connect and Communicate

When you make it easy for people to connect and collaborate, you encourage open communication as part of your core values. Tools like Zoom, Slack, and Skype are excellent ways to collaborate in real-time. I think that meetings in the virtual world where you combine gaming technology headsets with virtual rooms are going to become increasingly popular as the technology evolves and scales. Once you put on those headsets, you basically can't leave the room. Distractions are eliminated.

Freelancers often feel lonely and isolated. They can't share lunch breaks, go out for drinks, work out together, or converse in person with colleagues. If freelancers regularly communicate with each other, they're always informed about the latest news regarding their work. This means they'll be more productive. They don't have to communicate via video calls. They can always message each other. Tools companies use for communication usually offer more chats so that freelancers can have their non-work-related chat rooms.

Companies that encourage continuous communication are more time-efficient and productive with their work. As a result, their business is also a financial success. Freelancers can also set their apps to let people know when they're out of the office and when they'll return.

Cultural Issues

When you hire workers from another country or region, it's critical to understand the most effective way to communicate and to respect cultural differences and customs. Just as people in the U.S are going to be less likely to attend a meeting on Thanksgiving, people in the Philippines will want to be with families on the last Monday in August, National Heroes' Day. It's a day of parades, memorial services, and everyone is off work. Having a cultural calendar helps protect the private time your workers deserve and can help with your planning and scheduling.

> George, who owned an online retail business in the United States, expected his web designer, located many thousands of miles away, to provide updates and changes to the website on a moment's notice. Kabir, a web freelancer who supported the site, was very appreciative of the work, but reluctant to set boundaries with George for fear of losing his job. He understood the importance of making sure that George's website had the latest prices and products. When George contacted him, even in the middle of the night, Kabir felt compelled to respond immediately. His culture taught him that it was impolite to ever say "no" to a boss. This reluctance interfered with Kabir's relationship with his wife and caused him a lot of personal stress.

> When Laurie, one of George's customers, commented favorably about the recent

changes to George's website, George mentioned that he had one person in India who did everything for him 24x7. Laurie asked George to explain how that was possible with just one person. As their conversation continued, George began to realize that he had unreasonable expectations. George contacted Kabir and told him that he was a valued worker. George asked Kabir if having to be available on-demand was causing him any hardship and explained to Kabir that his job would not be in jeopardy if they adjusted his schedule to make it more accommodating. At that point, Kabir opened up to George, and they developed a new schedule that met George's expectations and made Kabir and his wife much happier.

chapter 9

Leveraging Tools and Best Practices

If you want to get the most value out of your free-lancers, having effective tools to manage and pay them is critical. But you need even more than that. You've got to have a flexible business model that supports the best practices you and your freelancers expect. After all, what good is it to simply have the technology if your fees are too high, or you can't attract the type of talent you need? How many freelancers are going to want to remain with you if you can't pay them quickly and efficiently in the currency of their choice? In this chapter, we'll describe what to expect from the technology you use and how this can impact your business.

Evaluating Freelance Websites

Let's pretend that you're in one of those Crime Scene Investigation (CSI) shows, and you have to do some profiling. What would be the profile of an ideal freelance website from a client's perspective? Follow these rules of thumb.

The best platform to hire freelancers should be absolutely free for clients. You don't pay when you post a project. You don't pay when your project is accepted, and there are no membership fees. You pay what you have to pay to your freelancer for a job properly done—no more and no less.

You should be able to save more as you spend more. What's that supposed to mean? Companies should appreciate your decision to spend money on their website and give you credit for economies of scale. That's why you should get some of your money back. How about a cash-back option for a change?

Just as you want to save money, you want to save time. For this purpose, it would be nice to use a time and activity tracker that gives you a quick overview of all work, so you don't have to go through work reports in detail. What I have in mind is a time/activity tracker with an activity success percentage. You see a percentage of activity on the screen for a particular day and can get an idea of the worker's productivity.

Your preferred freelance platform has to do its homework properly so that you can have peace of mind. All freelancers who apply to work on your project should go through a rigorous selection and verification process. The last thing you need is a freelance platform that wants to impress you with an overwhelming number of freelancers who may not have been verified.

You need a fair and equitable pricing model. Many freelance service fees are much too high. Freelance marketplaces have to be more equitable. Service fees for some marketplaces range from 10% to 20%, and this is too high. All additional costs, such as transfers and exchange fees, may not even be included. The clients have to pay the service fees too.

Third-party links for freelancers should be allowed so you have more data for evaluation. Some platforms have restrictions on using third-party links, even to the point of suspending accounts that include them. Freelancers should be allowed to attach Twitter, Quora, LinkedIn, or even their own website links to their accounts. This gives you a bigger-picture view of their background.

You should be able to easily locate freelancers if you want to use them again in the future. Here's another example of why transparency is so critical. A marketing consultant, Tim, had hired Anna, a designer, from a very large freelance marketplace to work on a project. When Tim wanted to hire Anna again several months later, he couldn't locate Anna's profile! Tim was overwhelmed by the thousands of other designers on the site, and it took him too much time to find and vet a replacement because that marketplace didn't link to third-party sites.

Legal and Ethical Responsibilities

The freelance economy should be a two-way street. Both parties, with the clients on one side and the freelancers on the other, should be happy about the outcome of their business relationships.

Clients and freelancers should reach an agreement about suitable prices for services. That decision shouldn't be made by the freelance marketplace company you choose. If you want to pay $50,000 to a freelancer and feel good about it, then why should your freelance marketplace judge this agreement? On the other hand, if a freelancer wants to do something at an unusually low rate for whatever reason, that's up to the freelancer to make that choice.

Freelancers have the absolute freedom to work on whichever platform they choose and decide what price to accept. They should also have the freedom to work on more than one company's platform at the same time.

Both the problem and the solution are in the freelancers' hands. When I was a freelancer, I used to have my minimum price. Now, as someone who hires freelancers and helps them find work, I leave it up to them to suggest a fair price. If this price is okay for me, then I give it a go. If not, I move on with my search.

Websites with International Freelancers

Many freelance websites claim that they're globally oriented, and all freelancers are welcome, no matter where they come from. However, if you scratch the surface and go through the registration and verification process, you quickly realize that it isn't entirely true.

I can't say that there's no discrimination, but there is "favorization." I had to play a bit with the words to come up with a nice rhyme for my point. I hope you don't mind. This means that some freelance platforms favor freelancers coming from certain countries. I won't say which platforms and countries go hand-in-hand as the most suitable freelance combination. If you freelance for some time, you'll figure it out yourself.

If you're serious about hiring the best talent at the best price, and you feel strongly about making the world a fairer place, you may want to avoid freelance platforms that are exclusionary. Watch for companies that say, "We're a platform for freelancers from India," "This is a European site," "The majority of our freelancers come from the USA," and so on. Labels and borders just don't go together in freelancing. If a platform is touted as an international freelance website, then it has to live up to its promise.

Effective Qualification Processes

A good online marketplace will take a holistic approach to match the right talent with the right opportunity. For example, the platform might use skills tests and cognitive tests. This involves encouraging freelancers to complete their profiles, include work samples, and take tests to certify their level of competency in specific areas. Also, it's vital to conduct one-on-one interviews for certain roles, to actively get to know freelancers, and make that extra effort to reach out and contact the most promising candidates.

Transparency between clients and freelancers is also critical. See if your potential platform lets its freelancers evaluate clients, and the clients to rate the freelancers on the website. This process makes it easy to verify skills to match clients with the best candidates for the jobs.

Freelancers can search through jobs worldwide on a well-designed platform, using various filters for skills, rates, and even locations. This capability should enable business customers and freelancers to have full transparency on payment rates. It's also helpful when freelancer data can also be synchronized with professional networks, such as

LinkedIn, and with testing capabilities that are integrated with a resource, such as Indeed Assessments.

Management and Payment Tools

When businesses hire freelancers, it's important to make it easy to manage workers from any location. Look for a provider that offers tools to record activities, track the time spent on an assignment, and communicate the status of projects. Having on-screen reporting makes it easier and much less expensive to manage remote workers than having to manage people sitting in an office.

By integrating a meter with payment applications from a variety of suppliers, freelancers can get electronic payments into their accounts quickly, based on their payment preferences.

Businesses that use global freelancers often require a variety of electronic payment options. An effective freelance platform should make this possible with low-cost exchange rates and pricing from numerous suppliers. That capability should be integrated with suppliers' solutions that help automate the entire payment process. This can include money transfers and digital payment services, as well as speedy, secure bitcoin services. Users should be able to access real-time exchange rates and have fast, secure, convenient, and lower-cost international transfers.

chapter 10

Trends in the Freelance Market

The future is remote and automated. So many careers can be advanced by remote online freelancers today. Of course, some services require direct physical interaction with customers or property. But even these can often be modified to function outside the constraints of a typical business. This became evident in April 2020, when a Gallup Report found that the percentage of Americans working from home had doubled since mid-March 2020 in response to the COVID-19 crisis. Nearly 60% of the people surveyed said they would prefer to work remotely as much as possible even after restrictions are lifted. (Source: Gallup, April 3, 2020, "U.S. Workers Discovering Affinity for Remote Work," Megan Brenan).

The Expanding Freelance Economy

The way companies produce products, deliver services, and interact with customers is changing before our eyes as our economy shifts to freelancing.

The minimum technical requirements for a job to become remote are simply having a computer, phone, and internet access — which almost everyone has. These basics are, in fact, about all you need for some of the most common online remote careers, namely writing, editing, photography, software development, website and graphic design, and virtual assistants. The only other requirements in freelancing are the specific skills needed to complete a job.

But what about traditional labor-intensive services such as automotive detailing or automotive repair? Freelance auto mechanics are already available that drive to your home and repair your car, instead of having you come into the shop.

We've seen how manual work has been reduced through computer-aided technology, and Numerical Control (CNC) technology has grown concurrently with computer technology. Machines are getting smaller, not bigger, and more affordable. Freelance designers and programmers are readily available.

Freelance machinists are supporting a variety of industries, such as the medical components sector. Machinists review programs, change cutting bits and move the position of a piece that's being worked on. Instead of paying a machine shop with overhead, businesses can outsource work to a freelancer. The only thing the freelancer needs is a machine and raw material. Once a product has been machined to exact tolerances, the freelancer can mail the customer a finished product. This eliminates minimum order requirements and fees associated with traditional machining work.

I suspect that there will be a vast range of freelancing jobs in the future for jobs that may not exist today. It has been widely quoted that an estimated 65% of the children entering primary school today will work in entirely new jobs that don't yet exist. While I can't predict what those jobs will be, I feel confident that there will be unprecedented opportunities for freelancers to work remotely.

Future Impacts

Automation will continue to reduce the costs of employment, increasing the demand for remote workers, and skilled freelancers. Consider how automation and remote workers have changed the movie rental industry. Instead of rental stores being on the corner of every street in America, movies are streamed online. Automated payments and digital delivery have eliminated the need for storefronts, employees, and massive inventories of movies. Customer support and service for companies that stream movies work in either a consolidated call center or work remotely from home. This helps reduce overhead.

Freelancing can also become more prominent in manually intensive careers. Service industries continue to become even more automated with the aid of robotic technology, limiting the skills necessary to perform jobs that require expert experience. The medical industry already uses robotic equipment to perform certain types of surgeries. The surgeon works from a remote terminal. So, if surgeons owned the right equipment, they could work on a freelance basis if they wanted to reach hospitals beyond their local areas. It is basically using the best available resources for the current requirements. Imagine if your elective surgery could be performed on the same day, instead of waiting weeks, because the surgeon that you need is currently available in another city, even though you may be 1,000 miles away from that doctor.

A Change Is Coming

Freelance work provides so much flexibility for businesses and talent and is no longer just a temporary position or a way to make ends meet. People are joining freelance marketplaces and finding other methods to work on a project-by-project basis instead of working a full-time job.

Here's an example of how people who are used to working in corporate positions may tend to gravitate to freelance opportunities because they appreciate the ability to work remotely and the chance to be their own boss:

> *Sarah worked as a senior marketing director and held various positions as a corporate employee for more than 15 years. She was well regarded in her company as an expert—someone who could solve just about any problem sent her way. When the company she worked for was acquired, there was a lot of uncertainty in her environment. She had six bosses in one year and struggled to get people to cooperate on her projects.*

123

When she was laid off during a major corporate reorganization, Sarah was actually relieved. She felt burnt out, disenfranchised, and ready to go out on her own. So, she became a freelancer. The companies that became her clients benefited from her vast knowledge and can-do approach. Sarah was happy because she felt more in control over her career and enjoyed the freedom of working for different clients and tackling new projects. Her story is becoming a very common one.

Freelancing is the best of both worlds, and the future *is* freelancing. There's something entrepreneurial in every freelancer. Freelancing isn't going to be the last resort, but rather the most logical choice for many people all over the world. Why? I've witnessed firsthand how the fine line between freelance and "regular" jobs fades away.

It is almost impossible to tell the difference between these two options. There are so many jobs you can do practically anywhere. This includes freelancers working for "traditional" companies and companies that have gone online and remotely almost to the last employee.

I dare to say that freelancing is the future, and the next logical step of our work-related evolution. I don't claim to know exactly what jobs will disappear, but I think even more advanced automation and freelance/remote workers will make a significant impact on the economy.

I foresee the future holding a vast majority of jobs from home or remote locations as opposed to office buildings, cubicles, or industrial parks. The cost benefits to both business leaders and freelancers will change the way we work, produce products, and live in general. Every day more people are signing up as freelancers on my platform and switching from their regular 9-to-5 jobs.

More and more businesses will realize that paying their employees 40 hours per week will result in higher costs due to various insurance policies, business overhead, and other expenses. Minimizing all of these standard costs will simultaneously allow businesses to increase their profits, and they'll also pay higher wages to the freelancers or remote employees.

I don't think jobs will disappear due to automation because there's always a need for skilled

experts in certain fields. Automation cannot replace human creativity, so writing, graphic and
website design, art, website design, software development, and other creativity-based skills and
trades will most likely rise in demand and cost. A
lot of jobs will be needed, but the primary changes
in the future will concern how these jobs are performed, what skills are required, and how human
involvement can be limited or minimized. I believe that these are all possibilities, based on our
current technology.

Conclusion

This is an exciting time for business owners who
have the freedom and flexibility of a remote workforce and technology to support it, none of which
were available at such an advanced level just a few
years ago. They can run their businesses from their
homes, beaches, or just about anywhere. They can
do this while watching their revenues grow, and
the administrative tasks associated with running a
business shrink due to increased efficiency.

Great technology, talent, business models, and a
thriving remote culture of world-class freelance
teams make this possible. You can achieve

business growth beyond your wildest expectations and win. Get started now. It's time to REMOTE iT!

REMOTE iT! Checklist

Are you ready to begin hiring freelance talent? Here is a checklist with some key questions and action items to help you get the results you need. Grab a notepad or start typing the answers to the questions below.

Identify what you need from a freelancer

1. What **skills** are you seeking from a freelancer? (Describe the type of work that this individual will perform.)

2. How much **experience** does this role require? (This will help you to determine how much to pay.)

3. What is the **project timeline**? (Identify how many hours you need to get the project completed and whether this will be an ongoing assignment.)

4. What is your **budget** for this project or role and how does it compare with what's offered elsewhere for this type of work?

5. If you hire a freelancer in a different time zone, what would be the most realistic and effective **working hours** for that person to be available?

6. Who will the freelancer **report to** and how will the freelancer's **work be measured**?

After answering questions 1-6, you should have enough information to write a brief project description and understand your requirements.

Verifying and interviewing the freelancer

7. What information can you glean from the **freelancer's digital profile** and work samples?

8. Have you been able to **verify the freelancer's work experience and references** and what are the results of the verification? (If you use an online platform that rates the freelancer, this can be very helpful. Also consider contacting some of the references.)

9. What **questions do you want to ask the freelancer** regarding this person's availability, work history, interest in the job, ability to

work remotely, expected compensation, experience working with teams, and any additional topics related to the position?

10. After interviewing this freelancer, on a scale of 1-10, with 10 being the best candidate and one being the least-likely candidate, **how do you rate this freelancer?** (This question will help you to identify the most likely person for the role.)

Questions 7 through 10 should help you to determine if the candidate meets your requirements.

Managing and paying the remote freelancer

11. How does the freelance platform you use help you **manage the work of a remote freelancer effectively**? (For example, does the time tracker take screen shots, include a work diary and provide an effective way to gain visibility into the time a worker spends on a particular task or project?)

12. How effective are the **payment capabilities** of the freelance platform you use? (Will the platform offer the freelancers the ability to be paid

in the currency of their choice? How quickly will they be paid?)

13. What is the **cost of using the freelance platform**? (Will the platform let you, as the hiring company, **use the platform without having to pay a fee**? Will the business model of the platform give you a **cash-back incentive** based on the amount of business conducted using that platform? Does the platform charge the freelancer a low fee?)

Questions 11 through 13 will help you identify the key characteristics of the technology and business model used to manage and pay freelancers. Freelancers will seek a platform that has low fees and can provide them with fast payments and quality jobs. As an entrepreneur, you can benefit from a platform that doesn't charge you fees to hire freelancers and is able to offer the skilled professionals you require.

Leading a great remote culture

14. Do you have the right technologies available to conduct remote meetings with your freelancer or freelance teams? (This includes document collaboration resources and video communication tools.)

15. What is your organization's mission statement and how do you plan to share that mission statement with your workers?

16. How do you plan to encourage open communication and digital friendships, as well as recognize the performance of key workers and teams?

Your response to questions 14 through 16 will help you build a strategy that can create a great remote culture with increased productivity and job satisfaction.

By answering these 16 questions, you should be in a great position to REMOTE iT!

For more information about hiring freelancers, visit golance.com.

REMOTE iT! Resources

Visit golance.com for:
Case studies
Blogs
FAQs
And more!

Facebook: facebook.com/golanceinc/
Twitter: twitter.com/goLanceInc
LinkedIn: linkedin.com/company/golance
Instagram: instagram.com/golanceofficial/

Acknowledgments

I'd like to thank my wife, Kali, for motivating me to always do my best and supporting my dream of building a freelance marketplace. My children have been very understanding and watched what it's like to run a freelance business and be an entrepreneur.

In addition, I really appreciate the dedicated team of goLancers who helped build and support the company. There are far too many names to mention here, but they are certainly appreciated, and I am forever grateful to them! Their outstanding efforts in development, design, administrative support, sales and marketing, writing, IT, and a variety of other areas have helped make goLance the thriving company it is today. Thanks to their remarkable skills and outstanding work ethic, we have made a difference in the lives of our freelancers and enabled our clients to grow their businesses.

I'd also like to thank the editors, Linda Donovan and Nebojsa Todorovic, for their efforts with this book. They helped me organize the information and expand upon some of the examples and tips.

Of course, I'd like to recognize the entire community of goLance freelancers, clients, and partners for their commitment to freelancing.

About The Author

Michael Brooks is the CEO and founder of goLance, an award-winning online freelance marketplace. He runs this company, which has about 550,000 users and $82 million in payouts (and growing), entirely on freelance talent. And he does this from his home or anywhere without the expense and office overhead of a traditional business.

Brooks is also the author of two books focused on digital currency and the credit card industry and has been a speaker at major global conferences on freelancing, remote work, digital currency, e-commerce, CRM automation, and other topics.

.